Thomas Jefferson

Declaring Our Freedom

Jeanne Dustman

Consultant

Glenn Manns, M.A.
Teaching American History Coordinator
Ohio Valley Educational Cooperative

Publishing Credits

Dona Herweck Rice, *Editor-in-Chief*; Lee Aucoin, *Creative Director*; Conni Medina, M.A.Ed., *Editorial Director*; Jamey Acosta, *Associate Editor*; Neri Garcia, *Senior Designer*; Stephanie Reid, *Photo Researcher*; Rachelle Cracchiolo, M.A.Ed., *Publisher*

Image Credits

cover Wikimedia; p.1 Wikimedia; p.4 Peale/Wikimedia; p.5 Jovannig/Shutterstock; p.6–7 Mr. T in DC/Flickr; p.8 Arsgera/Shutterstock; p.9 (top) John Keith/Shutterstock, (bottom) Library or Congress, LC-DIG-ppmsca-18191; p.10 Picture History/Newscom; p.11 Flight Collection/ Newscom; p.12 (left) Olemac/Shutterstock, (right) Library of Congress, LOC memory_0296; p.13 Picture History/Newscom; p.14 John Trumbull; p.15 Historical Documents Co.; p.16 Library of Congress; p.17 Matt McClain/Shutterstock; p.18 The Granger Collection; p.19 Library of Congress, LC-DIG-det-4a26387; p.20 Library of Congress, LC-USZC4-3254; p.21 Gary Paul Lewis/Shutterstock; p.22 Tim Bradley; p.23 Audrey Snider-Bell/Shutterstock; p.24 Seleznev Valery/Shutterstock; p.25 Pranav Vora/Shutterstock; p.26 Library of Congress, LC-USZC4-2474; p.27 (left) Library of Congress, (right) Library of Congress; p.28 (left) Library of Congress, LC-DIG-ppmsca-18191, (right) Historical Documents Co.; p.29 (left) Library of Congress, LC-USZC4-3254, (right) Vahamrick/Shutterstock

Teacher Created Materials
5301 Oceanus Drive
Huntington Beach, CA 92649-1030
http://www.tcmpub.com

ISBN 978-1-4333-1599-2

Printed by: 51497
Printed in: China

Table of Contents

A Great Leader 4
The Early Years 6
Lawyer's Life 10
Political Career 14
Home at Last 24
Let Freedom Ring 26
Time Line 28
Glossary 30
Index 31
Americans Today 32

A Great Leader

Thomas Jefferson was a great American. He served his country in many ways. He helped America become free from Great Britain (BRIT-en). He wrote laws that gave people more rights. Thomas was the third president of the United States.

Thomas Jefferson

Fun Fact

Thomas is one of the four American presidents on Mount Rushmore. Mount Rushmore celebrates the first 150 years of America.

Mount Rushmore

The Early Years

Thomas was born in Virginia (ver-JIN-yuh) on April 13, 1743. He lived on a **plantation**. A plantation is a large farm. His father was a farmer. His mother came from an important family.

Thomas's vegetable garden at his plantation called Monticello

Thomas loved to learn. He went to college for two years. He was a good student. He read many books. He studied for 14 hours each day! After college, Thomas studied law. He wanted to be a **lawyer** (LOI-er).

Fun Fact

Thomas was a good reader. He could read five languages!

Fun Fact

Thomas loved music. He played the violin.

Thomas went to the College of William and Mary in Virginia.

Lawyer's Life

Thomas was a very busy lawyer. He traveled around Virginia and met many people. They were ruled by the king of Great Britain. The people were not happy with the king's laws. They wanted to make their own laws. Thomas wanted to help them.

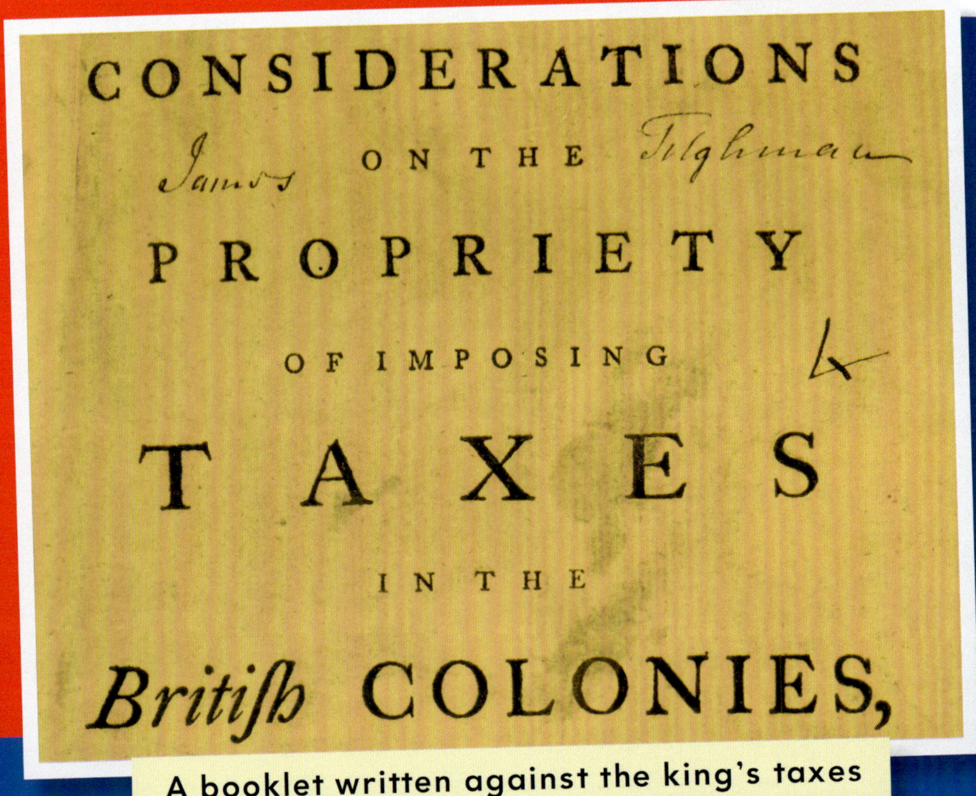
CONSIDERATIONS

ON THE

PROPRIETY

OF IMPOSING

TAXES

IN THE

British COLONIES,

A booklet written against the king's taxes

People were not happy about a tax on tea. They threw boxes of tea into the ocean. This is known as the Boston Tea Party.

Boston Tea Party

On the instructions given to the 1st delegation of Virginia to Congress in August 1774.

The legislature of Virginia happened to be in session in Williamsburg when news was recieved of the passage, by the British parliament, of the Boston port bill. this was to take effect on the 1st day of June then ensuing. the House of Burgesses thereupon past a resolution recommending to their fellow-citizens that that day should be set apart for fasting and prayer to the supreme being, imploring him to avert the calamities then threatening us, and to give us one heart and one mind to oppose every invasion of our liberties. the next day, May 20. 1774. the Governor dissolved us. we immediately repaired to a room in the Raleigh tavern, about 100. paces distant from the Capitol, formed ourselves into a Meeting, Peyton Randolph in the chair, and came to resolutions declaring that an attack on ne colony to enforce arbitrary acts, ought to be considered as an attac all, and to be opposed by the united wisdom of all. they therefore ointed a committee of correspondence to address letters to the Spea of the several Houses of Representatives of the Colonies, proposing the ap ment of deputies from each to meet annually in a General Congress, to rate on their common interests, and on the measures to be pursued mon. the members then separated to their several homes, except he Committee, who met the next day, prepared letters according to and dispatched them by messengers express to their several It had been agreed also by the Meeting that the Burgesses e elected under the writs ... m on a certain day in ... delegates to a Congr ... the election, the pe ... as a p ... their approbation ... to atten ... Convention, I pr ... him to the D ... who shoul ... proposed ... rawn in ...

Fun Fact

Thomas wrote about 20,000 (twenty thousand) letters in his lifetime!

Thomas was **elected** to the **House of Burgesses** (BUR-jis-is). The House of Burgesses was a group of men who made laws for Virginia. It was a good job for a lawyer. Thomas worked to get more **rights** for Americans. Thomas wrote letters to other leaders in the **colonies**. He wrote letters against the British laws.

A meeting at the House of Burgesses

Political Career

America went to war with Great Britain. America fought to be free. Thomas was a good writer. He was asked to write the **Declaration** (dek-luh-RAY-shuhn) **of Independence** (in-dih-PEN-duhns). This letter said that the colonies would not be ruled by Great Britain.

A meeting to show the Declaration of Independence to Congress

Declaration of Independence

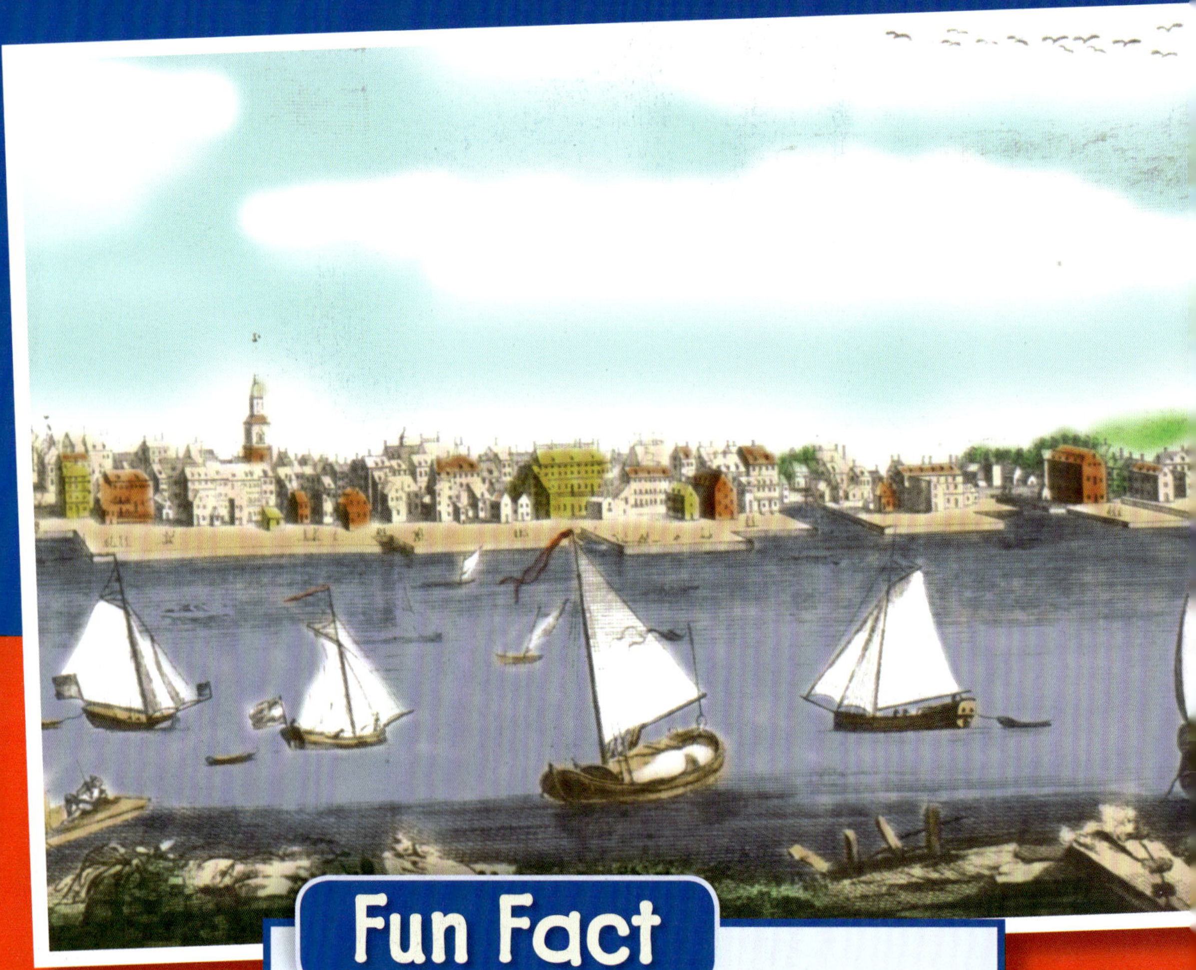

Fun Fact

Long ago people often traveled by ship. It took one month to get to France from America.

Thomas wanted to make life better for the people of Virginia. He wrote laws that gave people more freedom. More people could own land. People could choose their own churches. Thomas was elected **governor** (GUHV-er-ner) of Virginia.

Fun Fact

As governor of Virginia, Thomas lived in this special house.

Thomas got along well with people. He asked the king of France to trade with the colonies. President George Washington saw that Thomas was good at making deals. He asked him to be the first secretary of state.

President Washington with his team of leaders

Secretary of State
Thomas Jefferson

In 1796, Thomas ran for president of the United States. But he did not win. John Adams won. Thomas became vice president. In 1800, he ran again and won. He was the third president of the United States.

A painting of Thomas

Fun Fact

Thomas designed his home. He called it Monticello. He loved his home.

Let Freedom Ring

Thomas was a great leader. He helped America win its freedom. He wrote laws to give people more freedom. Thomas died on July 4, 1826.

A painting of Thomas

Fun Fact

Thomas and his friend John Adams died on the same day.

Thomas Jefferson

John Adams

Time

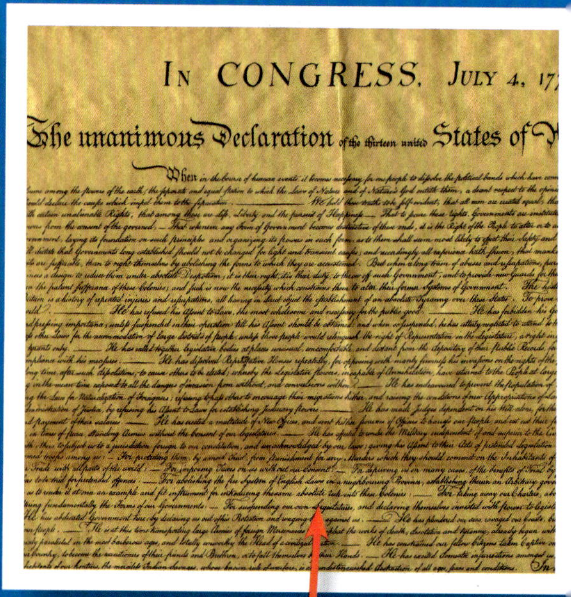

1743
Thomas Jefferson is born in Virginia.

1760 1762
Thomas attends college.

1775
Thomas writes the Declaration of Independence.

Line

1800

Thomas is elected president of the United States.

1819

Thomas starts the University of Virginia.

1826

Thomas dies at the age of 83.

Glossary

colonies—countries or areas that are ruled by a more powerful country

Declaration of Independence—a formal paper that said the 13 American colonies were free from Great Britain

elected—chosen for a job by voting

governor—a person in charge of a state government

House of Burgesses—the first government of the American colonies

lawyer—a person whose job is to tell people about the law and to speak for them in court

Library of Congress—one of the world's largest collections of books

plantation—a large farm where crops are grown

president—a person who is the leader of a government

rights—what the law allows people to do, or what the law should allow people to do

secretary of state—a person in charge of working with other countries

Index

Adams, John, 20, 27
Boston Tea Party, 11
College of William and Mary, 9
Declaration of Independence, 14–15
France, 16, 18, 22
Great Britain, 4, 10, 14
House of Burgesses, 13
Lewis and Clark, 22–23
Library of Congress, 24
Louisiana Territory, 22
Monticello, 7, 25
Mount Rushmore, 5
secretary of state, 18–19
University of Virginia, 24
Virginia, 6, 9–10, 13, 17, 24
Washington, George, 18

Americans Today

Hillary Clinton was chosen as the secretary of state in 2008. As secretary of state, she travels around the world and meets with world leaders. Hillary works to help countries get along. She helps keep peace in the world.